D0642910

"FOLLOW YOUR DREAMS"
SECRETS TO GETTING HIRED AS A FLIGHT ATTENDANT

Health and Beauty Tips You Must Know

PLUS

"How I Survived The New York Trade Center Bombing"

By Tammy Clark

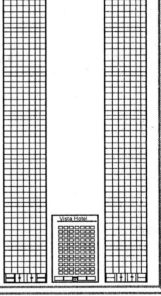

Vista Hotel

BH 9/65

ISBN: 0-7596-6352-1 (e-book)
ISBN: 0-7596-6353-X (Paperback)

This book is printed on acid free paper.

1stBooks - rev. 12/12/02

Tables of Contents

<u>Acknowledgement</u>

A special thank you to my sister Susan Sayer for assisting in the editing process and to my husband Vince Clark for his help and support.

Introductory

If you have the desire to become a flight attendant, the first thing I want to say is "Don't give up!" Believe it or not, getting the job as a flight attendant is very difficult. Everyday the airlines receive thousands of applications and it is imperative that your application gets noticed. You'll be up against the "Cream of the Crop" and "The Best of the Best." That's why I am writing this book, to help you achieve your dreams as a flight attendant.

I began interviewing in 1982 and continued these interviews until 1989. My first interview was with Republic Airlines. I was twenty-two years old and truthfully not ready for what I was trying to achieve and believe me, they knew it. Soon after, I was notified that the position was not available. That interview was just the beginning for me because this was the first of many. By the time I was through, I had interviewed with all of the major airlines.

In December of 1989 I decided to give up my pursuit of becoming a flight attendant. The pressure of trying so hard to get the job and then being denied was overwhelming. My mind was made up, I told my family and friends that I was never going to interview again.

Two weeks later, a flight attendant from Delta Airlines came into the department store where I was employed. As I assisted her, we began to discuss the flight attendant career. I will never forget the inspiration she gave me when she told me not to give up. She offered to bring me an application the following week, to my surprise she did. Because of her words of inspiration, I completed the application that evening and mailed it the following day. Two weeks later ... my personal invitation for an interview arrived by mail. Soon after, I was hired! Believe me when I tell you, your dreams can come true. So, do as I did and "Follow Your Dreams."

CHAPTER I

Job Application

TAMMY CLARK

The application process is the first step in the hiring process. A well-completed application will get the attention of the person reviewing your paperwork, and will forward it to the next level of the hiring process.

Do not type your application! The reviewers prefer that you fill out your application in black ink and in your own hand writing. They want to see how well you write due to the amount of paper work (i.e., Liquor, Passenger and Flight reports) that needs to be done throughout each flight. It's imperative that you complete the form and do so neatly.

Always write the truth! Never lie on your application. I have personally seen what can happen when you are not completely truthful. There were students dismissed from my training class because they lied on their application.

Once you have completed your paperwork, attach a recent picture of yourself that is conservative. The airlines love this idea because it gives them the opportunity to see you first hand. This will definitely expedite your interview process.

Also expect specific questions on your application such as, Question: Why do you want to be a flight attendant?
Your Answer: Try and give a unique answer. Give it some thought because if your answer is typical (*I love people, because I love flying or because I want to travel*) you won't get noticed. My suggestion is something along the lines of; *I WELCOME THE CHALLENGE AND OPPORTUNITY THE FLIGHT ATTENDANT POSITION WOULD GIVE ME. BECOMING A FLIGHT ATTENDANT WOULD ALLOW ME TO UTILIZE MY SKILLS IN COMMUNICATION WITH THE PASSENGERS.* I ENJOY WORKING WITH PEOPLE AND FEEL THAT I WOULD MAKE AN EXCELLENT FLIGHT ATTENDANT. This is just an example of the kind of answer a reviewer may

look for. After you have mailed your application, expect to hear back in a couple of weeks for a possible interview.

In most cases, the airlines will fly you to their headquarters for the interview if you don't live in the immediate area. How's that for incentive, fly free before your hired.

How to apply with Delta Airlines: You must be at least 20 years of age, high school graduate willing to relocate. You must successfully complete Delta's five week training course in Atlanta. You also need to maintain a 90% average during training. Delta employees enjoy their excellent compensation and benefits package.

The Following information was "Pasted" from various Airlines Website.

delta.com

Flight Attendant
Delta Flight Attendants - The best in the sky

They're a big part of why people love flying Delta Air Lines. We are currently **NOT HIRING** Flight Attendants.

Although Delta Air Lines is not currently recruiting for opportunities in the Initial Flight Attendant Training Course, please continue to visit our site for the latest Flight Attendant career information.

All individuals interested in becoming a Delta Flight Attendant must first qualify by being accepted to and completing the Delta Air Lines Initial Flight Attendant Training Course. In addition, people interested in pursuing a Flight Attendant career must have excellent customer service skills, be at least 20 years of age, have a high school diploma or GED, and be willing to relocate.

If you are selected as a trainee to participate in the Initial Flight Attendant Training Course, you will undergo five weeks of tuition-free training at Delta's Training Center in Atlanta. Students who successfully complete the training course will receive a training expense reimbursement of $500 for expense incurred during the five week training period. Some meals will be provided. Classes and training flights may be conducted seven days a week. The training is intensive and covers areas such as

5

government rules and regulations, emergency procedures, customer service, and Delta's policies and guidelines. Tests are given frequently and students must maintain an average of 90% in order to continue in the training program.

Training course students are not considered employment applicants for flight attendant positions until such time as they have successfully completed training and are invited to apply for employment when flight attendant positions become available. Successful completion of the course does not guarantee employment or an invitation to apply for employment.

Delta flight attendants are currently based in Atlanta, Boston, Chicago, Cincinnati, Dallas, Houston, Los Angeles, Miami, New Orleans, New York, Orlando, Portland (Oregon), Sale Lake City, and Seattle. If you are employed by Delta, you must be willing to relocate to any one of Delta's bases in accordance with Delta's operational needs. New flight attendants are on reserve for a period following their employment and are on call on a 24-hour basis to report for duty with little notice.

Note: Delta only accepts resumés and applications for admission to the Initial Flight Attendant Training Course when opportunities are available. Resumés and Applications received for opportunities not currently available will be discarded.

We are currently **NOT HIRING** flight Attendants.

How to Apply

Delta Air Lines vision is to become the world's greatest airline. Our mission is to build an airline operated by people whose commitment to service ensures that customers will always choose to fly Delta. **Delta only accepts resumés for positions which are available at the time of submission.** Available positions and corresponding Job Numbers are displayed in this web site. If a position does not have a Job Number, then it is a description only and not a current opening. Accordingly, when a position is available, submit your resumé, specifically indicating the Job Number for the position of your interest, either on your resumé or in a cover letter. Resumés received without a clearly stated Job Number for the available position of interest will be discarded.

Send your resumé, including the specific Job Number:

Via Email (preferred)
As text in the body of an email message (resumés sent as attachments cannot be accepted) to: **delta.careers@delta.com**

or

Via US Mail
Delta Air Lines, Inc.
Recruitment and Employment Office
P. O. Box 20530
Atlanta, GA 30320-2530

As an equal opportunity employer, Delta Air Lines, Inc. encourages workforce diversity. We recognize that by promoting the unique ideas and experiences of each individual, Delta positions itself as a company poised for continued growth in a rapidly changing global community.

▲**Delta**
delta.com

Resume Tips
Optimize Your Resume

To be the best airline in the world, Delta begins with a world class recruiting and selection process. Accordingly, Delta is incorporating the latest technology into the candidate qualifications review process. At Delta, we use a scannable resume reader, which allows the computer to read multiple pages at one time. We then use all the information it extracts from your resume to determine if your skills match any available positions. In addition, it allows you to provide more information than you would for a human reader.

To receive superior results from Delta's resume reading technology, however, we recommend that you use the following guidelines to construct your resume:

- Use white or light-colored 8 ½ x 11 paper, printed on one side only.

- Provide a laser printed or typewritten original if possible. Avoid dot matrix printouts and low quality copies.

- Do not fold or staple.

- Use standard typefaces: Helvetica, Futura, Optima, Univers, Times (avoid Times 10 point), Palatino, New Century Schoolbook, and Courier.

- Use a font size of 10 to 14 points.

- Do not condense spacing between letters.

- Use boldface and/or all capital letters for section headings as long as the letters do not touch each other.

- Avoid fancy treatments such as italics, underline, vertical and horizontal lines, graphics, boxes, shadows, and reverses (white letters on black background).

- Avoid a two-column format or resumes that look like newspapers or newsletters.

- Place your name at the top of the page on its own line. (Your name can also be the first text on pages two and three).

- Use the following standard address format below your name: name; address; city, state and zip code.

- List each phone number on its own line.

- Describe your skills, experience, education, and professional affiliations with concrete words rather than vague descriptions. For example, it's better to use "managed a team of software engineers" than "responsible for managing, training..."

- Only use jargon and acronyms specific to your specialty (spell out the acronyms for human readers).

- Increase your list of key words by including specifics, for example, list the names of software you use such as Microsoft Word, PowerPoint and Lotus 1-2-3.

- Use common headings such as: Objective, Experience, Employment, Work History, Positions Held, Appointments, Skills, Summary, Summary of Qualifications, Accomplishments, Strengths,

Education, Affiliations, Professional Affiliations, Publications, Papers, Licenses, Certifications, Examinations, Honors, References, etc.

Describe your interpersonal traits and attitude, if space allows. Key words could include skill in time management, dependable, high energy, leadership, sense of responsibility, good memory, etc.

UNITED

As one of the world's largest airlines, United brings people to hundreds of destinations around the globe each day. Many passengers base their impression of United on the service they receive onboard our flights. By providing the highest levels of safety and service, our flight attendants greatly impact the experience.

Duties

As a United Airlines flight attendant, you are responsible for the safety and comfort of our passengers. Your duties will include food and beverage service, assisting passengers with baggage, helping ill passengers or passengers with disabilities, answering inquiries, and operating mechanical and safety equipment.

Minimum qualifications

A neat, conservative and well-groomed appearance is essential for the look of a true professional. In addition, you must:

- Be at least 19 years old
- Have vision correctable to 20/30 (Neither eye can be worse than 20/100 uncorrected for people who wear glasses, or worse than 20/200 for contact lenses users)
- Possess a valid passport prior to training
- Have the legal right to accept full-time employment in the U.S. and for multiple entries and exits for all countries United serves

- Not exceed 6 feet 2 inches (1.83 meters) in height and have a minimum vertical reach of 82 inches (2.08 meters)

- Be willing to relocate to any of our 13 U.S. domiciles

- Possess a high school diploma or G.E.D.

- Have experience involving customer service

Selection and training

The selection process involves two interviews. The initial interview is conducted at one of the major cities served by United. The most competitive candidates are invited to our World Headquarters in Chicago for final evaluation. Prior to training, candidates must successfully complete a physical examination, background check, a three-week home study program and a pre-test.

Those selected for training must successfully complete a six-week, tuition free training program at our Flight Attendant Training Center in suburban Chicago, Illinois. Free room and board are provided. Training includes classroom work, homework and training flights. Some of the topics covered are aircraft equipment familiarization, food and beverage service, emergency procedures and first aid.

Relocation

Upon completion of training, graduates are assigned to one of our domestic domiciles - Boston, Chicago, Denver, Honolulu, Las Vegas, Los Angeles, Miami, Newark, New York, Philadelphia, San Francisco, Seattle or Washington, D.C. Domicile preference is not always available. You must be willing to relocate. Flight Attendants are eligible to request a transfer after six months to any other domicile, including

Frankfurt, London, Hong Kong, Paris, Santiago, Taipei and Tokyo.

Reserve

All new flight attendants are assigned to reserve flying. That means you must be able to fly at all times when you're "on-call," often with as little as four hours notice. Reserve flight attendants receive a minimum of 12 days off each month. Seniority at the domicile determines how long a flight attendant will be assigned to reserve flying. New flight attendants should expect to fly reserve for the first several years of employment.

Salary

Flight attendants are represented by the Association of Flight Attendants (AFA) and our flight attendant contract is widely recognized as the best in the industry. Your salary is established by the AFA contract in effect at the time of your employment. In general, flight attendants are paid based on the number of hours they fly per month, and their years of service. In addition to your base pay, cost-of-living adjustments, holiday pay, reserve override and ground pay, you will also be paid expense money for each hour you are away from your home base. When your flight involves layovers, lodging is always provided by United.

Come join the airline that's uniting the world! Come join United Airlines!

United Airlines is an Equal Opportunity Employer, m/f/d/v.

Copy of online opening:

LUV to be a Southwest Airlines Flight Attendant?

Interviews are conducted in the following cities:

- Baltimore, MD
- Chicago, IL
- Dallas, TX
- Houston, TX
- Oakland, CA
- Orlando, FL
- Phoenix, AZ

<u>**Send us your resume***</u> **today to get invited to an interview!**
*Resumes are held on file for six months.

<u>**What It Takes to Be a Flight Attendant at SWA**</u>
☐

- Locations
- Summary of Essential Job Functions
- Qualifications and Requirements
- Pay

☐
<u>**Hiring Process**</u>
☐
<u>**Why Become a Southwest Airlines Flight Attendant?**</u>

- Employee Benefits
- Quotes From Our Very Own Flight Attendants

What It Takes to Be a Flight Attendant at SWA

TAMMY CLARK

Flight Attendants provide legendary Customer Service on board the aircraft by performing safety, passenger service, and cabin preparation duties.

SUMMARY OF ESSENTIAL JOB FUNCTIONS:

- Responsible for providing legendary Customer Service to passengers desiring to travel by performing or assisting in the performance of all safety, passenger service, and cabin preparation duties.

- Provides Customers with safety information to ensure onboard safety compliance with government and Company regulations.

- Provides leadership, direction, and assistance during an emergency, including aircraft evacuation, administering first aid to ill or incapacitated Customers, and unusual incidents (bomb threats, hijackings, delayed flights, severe weather conditions, turbulent flights, etc.)

- Assists passengers with carryon items. Occasionally lifts carryon items from floor to above shoulder level with assistance to secure cabin for takeoff and landing.

- Has the ability to lift cabin equipment weighing 50 pounds from floor to above shoulder level as required. Serves beverages and snacks to Customers, collecting appropriate cash or coupon payments for alcoholic beverages and accounting for such receipts.

- Working environment subject to varying climate conditions, air turbulence, changing locations, variable hours and working conditions, dry air, noise levels from engines and other ground equipment, dim lighting, confined spaces and continuous and frequent contact with others.

- Works under hazardous conditions handling emergencies.

- Works in aircraft aisles and galleys, standing, reaching (extended in front of body and above head), walking, kneeling, and stooping for periods of long duration, and sitting for takeoff and landing.

- Works independently without constant supervision and observation.

- Work must be performed in accordance with established guidelines, procedures, and performance standards.

- Reads and interprets service and emergency instructions and communicates information to Customers and Crew.

- Operates mechanical equipment and safety equipment to include: stairs, oxygen systems, aircraft doors (pushing and pulling), evacuation slides, fire extinguishers, life rafts, galley equipment, communications equipment, and lighting systems.

- Other duties may be assigned from time to time.

QUALIFICATIONS AND REQUIREMENTS:

- Must be at least 20 years of age.

- High School diploma or equivalency required.

- College course or degree would be an asset.

- Mental capacity to read documents, follow instructions, learn and understand emergency and Company procedures, rules and regulations.

- Must have ability to comprehend and keep abreast of information pertinent to the job such as special promotions and new procedures.

- Must successfully complete initial and recurrent training programs.

- Must be aware of hazardous situations and be able to provide a leadership role in emergencies as needed.

- Works under tight time constraints to assure service on flights of short duration and quick turnaround of flights and on-time departures.

- Ability to work well with others as part of a team, excellent verbal communications and interpersonal skills.

- Must have ability to work well with the public on a constant basis under stressful conditions.

- A well-groomed appearance is required. Weight must be of such proportion to height that a neat appearance is maintained and physical ability to perform all functions is not hindered. The ability to, while facing forward, walk and fit comfortably down the aircraft aisle, fit quickly through the overwing window exit, and to fit into a jumpseat harness without modification, including closure without a seatbelt extension.

- Must be able to lift of up to 50 pounds from floor to above shoulder level as required. Also requires the ability to lift carryon items from floor to above shoulder level with assistance.

- Foreign language skills preferred, but not required.

- Ability to work rotating shift work, and/or overtime and travel on a constant basis. Must be able to comply with Company attendance standards described in labor agreements and/or established guidelines. Will be required to work "Junior Available" and Reserve Flight Attendant" depending on seniority.

- Must be a U.S. citizen or have authorization to work in the U.S. as defined in the Immigrations Act of 1986.

PAY:

1st 6 Months	2nd 6 Months	2nd Year
$14.67/Trip*	$14.90/Trip	$17.34/Trip

*one trip = 243 miles

All pay rates are contingent upon current contracts

Back to Top

Hiring Process

1. Submit a resume.

2. Attend a Group Information/Screening Session.

3. Attend a one-on-one Interview and **complete an application** (if recommended from the Group to continue in the interview process).

4. Background check (if recommended from one-on-one to continue the interview process).

5. Drug screening.

6. Successfully complete phases 4 and 5.

7. Invited to Flight Attendant Training Class; completion required before becoming a Flight Attendant.

<u>Back to Top</u>

Why Become a Southwest Airlines Flight Attendant?
Did You Know . . .

- All SWA Employees and their eligible family members have FREE UNLIMITED space available travel anywhere Southwest Airlines flies!

- As a SWA Employees you will receive Profit Sharing. . . and Southwest Airlines has had 29 consecutive years of profit!

- Southwest Airlines has FABULOUS Medical, Dental and Vision plans for all Employees!

- SWA offers a casual uniform environment, which means you can wear tennis shoes!

- The Southwest Airlines University offers Career Development classes for all SWA Employees!

- Southwest Airlines holds Chili Cookoffs, Holiday Celebrations, Deck Parties, Golf Tournaments and more for all SWA Employees and their family members.

- SWA Employees get a dollar for dollar match in their 401K - up to 6.3% of their investment!

Get more information on <u>Southwest Airlines Employee Benefits</u>

Quotes From Our Very Own Flight Attendants. . .

"The freedom to make your own schedule. Work as much or as little as you want. No more road rage!! See the country. Meet awesome people and become a part of our big SWA family. Enjoy the freedom to have fun and be yourself." -- Vicki Simmons

"Think of this as an adventure not just a job." -- Travis

"Fun! Fun! Fun! What a great job! Go for the best - fly with Southwest" -- Sandy Collard

"Working for SWA is being able to color outside the lines, being able to be yourself and have fun!!" -- Vicki Simmons

☐

Interview Tips

- Be on time (we are the on-time carrier), know where you are going ahead of time.
- Dress accordingly (after all this is your interview - business attire is recommended).
- Allow ample time for your interview.
- Turn your electronic devices to the off position.
- Don't chew gum.

<u>Back to Top</u>

☐

Uniforms - From Hot Pants to Polo Shirts; From Go-Go Boots to Tennis Shoes … My How We've Changed!

What to Bring …

When you arrive at your interview, you may be asked to fill out a Southwest Airlines application. In order to assist you in completing the application,

PLEASE BRING the following information/documents with you to the interview:

Employment History:	For the past 10 years or back to the age of 18 (whichever is shorter). Include company name, address and telephone number. Provide the month and year of employment and position held.
Residence Addresses:	For the past 10 years or back to the age of 18 (whichever is shorter). Include zip codes with month and year. We cannot have **ANY** gaps. (Forgotten zip codes may be obtained by calling 1-800-ASK-USPS.)
Education:	Name, address, and telephone number of high school or college attended.
Unemployment: (6 months or longer)	Periods of unemployment of 6 months or longer must be listed with month and year along with the names and telephone numbers of 2 personal references (NOT RELATIVES).

In addition to the above, please provide a **COPY** of the following documents **enclosed in a sealed envelope**:

☐
Your Driver's License

☐
Your high school diploma, GED or college diploma if applicable

☐
DD214-Member 4 (if you have been in the military in the last 5 years)

If any of the above information is incomplete on your application, consideration for employment may be delayed or discontinued.

Call our Job Hotline:

Dallas: (214) 792-4803
Phoenix: (602) 389-3738
Southwest Airlines, an Equal Opportunity Employer.

These are the airlines that I believe are the best in the Industry. If you prefer to venture out on your own, I wish you the best of luck!

TAMMY CLARK

<u>CHAPTER II</u>

Personal Appearance

TAMMY CLARK

Now it's time to get in shape for the interview! I recommend that you follow my health tips and beauty secrets before you attend your interview. The airlines expect you to look perfect and will observe you closely during the interviewing process. They will look at your weight, skin, hair, nails, teeth, makeup, clothing and how well you're put together.

Now let's have some fun! Choosing the right kind of make up for my female readers.

At your interview you should wear foundation, blush, eyeliner, eye shadow and lipstick. Don't wear heavy makeup on your eyes. If your eyes are blue you should wear brown, honey or bronze eye shadow; these colors will get your eyes noticed! If your eyes are brown you should wear burgundy, gold or jade eye shadow. Apply very lightly.

Choose a foundation that matches your skin, so that you look natural. Accent your cheeks with colors such as, honey, rose, bronze, pale pink or red.

American Airlines loves the Mary Tyler Moore look! It appears that they like red lipstick, nails and cheeks. In contrast Delta Airlines loves pretty in pink, the sweet southern girl image. So adjust yourself when you go to the interview.

- Wear red blush lightly. Red is a beautiful color to wear on your cheeks and lips, if you keep it natural.

- Wear lipstick that matches your blush. Apply vitamin e over your lipstick for natural shine and healthy lips.

- Use vitamin e on your eyelashes instead of mascara. Your eyelashes will appear lush and long.

27

- Reapply vitamin e for a fresh natural look all the time.

Gentlemen:

You too must capture the look! Here's what you need to do.

- Your hair should be styled conservatively and should be of natural color. Never color your hair for an interview.

- It's best to have no facial hair or ear piercings. You should not wear cologne. Your interviewer could have an allergic reaction. That's the last thing you want to happen!

- Wear a navy suit with a white shirt underneath and select a tie that looks patriotic! Choose a simple design with colors such as, red, blue and gold.

- Don't forget to polish your shoes and wear dark colors such as, black, brown or burgundy.

- For the finishing touch place a hanker-chief in the pocket of your jacket. You're ready to go!

Health:

If you are struggling with your weight and/or skin I highly recommend you follow my daily health routine. My daily ritual will help you loose weight and clear your skin up if you have minor acne.

Follow Your Dreams Daily Ritual:

Prepare your skin for the morning.

Wash your face with a mild cleanser and toner. Break open a vitamin e capsule and mix it with your eye-cream. Apply directly under your eye to prevent wrinkles. I suggest that you wear a face cream instead of lotion. Cream holds up better to the elements. For extra moisture mix vitamin e with your face cream and apply to your face and neck. If you have light acne, apply 100% aloe-vera gel right on the pimple. This will help heal the pimple and dry it out naturally. It will also help prevent future breakouts.

 Breakfast:

Find a special place in your house where you can enjoy a cup of coffee. This should be a place that makes you feel alive and energized. I have a special place in my living room where I enjoy my coffee in the morning. After I drink my coffee and prepare my thoughts for the day, I help myself to a tall glass of instant breakfast, using non-fat milk. I don't recommend eating heavy in the morning. If you need more in your stomach, I suggest eating fruit, yogurt or muffins. Never eat greasy foods in the morning.

Now that you have completed your morning ritual, wait an hour for your food to digest then get ready to exercise.

 Stretch! Stretch! Stretch! Most people forget to do this. That's how injuries occur.

 Find a place to exercise that makes you feel good.

EXERCISE REGIMINE:

➥ Stand up right and spread your legs slightly.

➥ Put your hands in the air and bend from side to side slowly.

➥ Stretch your midsection. (Start with ten on each side).

➥ Standing upright stretch your arms by moving them in a circular motion, stretching your shoulders.

➥ Bend your body and touch your toes. (If you can't touch your toes just bend as far as you can to stretch your back and legs). Remember this should be done slowly so that you don't injure yourself!

➥ Lay down and pull your legs toward you, stretching your lower back.

➥ Stand with your legs slightly apart. Put your arms straight out by your side, then twist slowly.

➥ Get a chair and place your hands on the back of the chair.

➥ Lift your leg backward and stretch the buttock muscles. (Do as many as you can on each leg).

➥ Lift your leg sideways up and down holding the back of the chair.

➥ Sit upright in the chair, placing your feet on the ground.

➥ Lift your leg up and down.

Do repetitions for each leg to build the muscles in your upper leg.

Now that you're all stretched out it's time to dance! If you want a pretty stomach you have to move your midsection. Put on your favorite music and prepare for aerobic style dancing. **Follow your dreams style dancing!**

➢ Dance to the music by moving your midsection in a circular motion, like your belly dancing. Raise your arms and move them in a circular motion as you move your midsection.

➢ Move your hips from side to side while you move your arms up and down as if you were reaching for the sky.

➢ Bend your arms up towards your chest clutching your fists then twist your upper body as you step to the side with your foot. Example: Your upper body turns to the left as your right foot takes a step to the right side, then your upper body turns to the right as your left foot steps out to the left.

➢ Bend your arms towards your chest in a boxing style then jab forward and move your hips from side to side.

➢ You should make the exercise steps like a dance.

Warm Down:

Continue to dance any style you want to as you slow your movements down. Take a deep breath and exhale. Put your arms in the air slowly stretching from side to side. Lift your leg

31

backward stretching your buttocks, then stretch your arms out and twist your midsection.

Get a towel and go to the sink. Do push- ups on the ledge of the sink if you have a base to put your hands on. This will build your arms and chest muscles. Then you can work your way up in strength. Test your arm strength by doing a few push-ups on the sink. This way you can find a good distance to place your feet on the floor where you will be comfortable while exercising.

Now that you have successfully completed your work out, it's time for a refreshing beauty smoothie.

If you are having trouble with your complexion, my homemade beauty smoothie will clear up minor acne. If your skin has serious acne consult a dermatologist.

BEAUTY SMOOTHIE
　　2 cups ice
　　Handful of parsley
　　Handful of fresh blueberries

3 baby carrots
4 large strawberries
½ apple
½ banana
½ cup strawberry margarita mix (non-alcoholic)
½ cup orange juice
1 cup milk
1-2 scoops of vanilla ice cream or yogurt

Directions:

Fill your blender with ice. Then take the tops of the parsley and wash them with cold water. Note: all of the fruits and vegetables can be thrown in whole after you cut them. Wash your baby carrots, strawberries, and apple. Cut the top and bottom off of the strawberries. Cut the apple and pealed banana in half and put in blender. Pour half cup of strawberry mix, orange juice and one cup of milk into the blender. Add two scoops of vanilla ice cream.

 Lunchtime:

Steam broccoli and serve with pasta. I highly recommend eating broccoli everyday. You will see an improvement in your skin. Broccoli is an anti-oxidants, it also fights cancer. For best results steam your broccoli or eat it raw. Eat broccoli with all your lunch meals and if you get tired of it, eat asparagus. Combine broccoli in with rice for an energy meal. Use brown rice instead of white. Brown rice keeps you young, while white rice ages you. Don't eat meat during the day. Stick with vegetables, pasta, rice or beans in the afternoon. I recommend a multi-vitamin with your lunch. Take vitamins daily with plenty of water (you should drink at least eight glasses per day) and your skin will start to look better.

In the late afternoon, drink a fresh cup of coffee or tea. This is the time to find another special place where you enjoy sitting. Light a candle, enjoy crumb cake (or any dessert you want) with your coffee. Don't snack after this!

 Dinnertime:

Prepare your meal: Cook meat, vegetables, and a side dish. Keep your portions small and don't go back for seconds. Please help yourself to lasagna, macaroni or any dish that you love. Believe it or not you may eat dessert! It's your choice! If you follow this daily planner, your health will improve and your weight will decrease. Always, consult your doctor before changing your diet.

Hair:

Wear your hair up and away from your face. For a classic look, style your hair in a French twist. Keep it simple and natural. Let me share with you my secret to beautiful hair. Try my homemade banana conditioner! Your hair will love you!

Recipe:

1 cup of purified water
1-2 banana's
1 table spoon of lemon juice
1 capsule of vitamin e
½ cup of orange juice

In a blender mix ingredient's together. Put blender on high and mix well. Add water if too thick.

♦ Wash your hair with your favorite shampoo and rinse well. Apply conditioner; rub gently into scalp and hair.

- Rinse hair extremely well! Make sure all the conditioner is out of your hair.

- If you have a favorite conditioner apply after banana treatment.

- Mist your hair with a light leave-in conditioner.

- Apply gel and style.

Your hair should be full of body, luster and shine. For best results, use once a week or on special occasions. This will eliminate build up.

You can do this! Just be natural and confident and I'm sure you will shine at your interview.

TAMMY CLARK

<u>CHAPTER III</u>

The Interview

TAMMY CLARK

This section will give you a good example of what to expect at your first interview. Although I went on my interview in 1990, I'm sure the interview process is basically the same. Every company has their own technique of interviewing however, my experience and recommendations are great for information at your interview.

Prepare for the interview:

I recommend making arrangements to arrive one day prior to the interview. The airlines will fly for free to the location of the interview and may even pay for your hotel room. Usually interviews begin very early in the morning and last long into the day, so bring your munchies!

Some interviews have between 20-30 applicants sitting together in what's called the "Group Interview." The group interview is usually the first step. This is your opportunity to get noticed and stand out in some way to the panel of interviewers. No doubt about it, the interview is one of the most nerve-racking processes you will ever go through.

How to answer questions in a group interview:

The first thing to do is to take a deep breath, concentrate and focus in on what you're about to do. Don't worry about what you're going to say to the interviewers (they'll be looking for things such as; how you're sitting in the chair, eye contact, and confidence and how well you communicate with them). If they ask you questions such as <u>Why do you want to be a flight attendant?</u>

- ♦ Smile and say you would be honored to be one of their flight attendants.

- Tell them you would be a faithful employee.

- Explain that you love working with people.

- Look at them in the eyes when you talk. Be sincere about what you're saying.

- Smile at the interviewers and charm them.

The interviewers are trained to recognize these attributes so don't appear shy or scared.

The interviewers may ask you, <u>Why would you make a good flight attendant?</u>

- Look the interviewer in the eyes and say: I would make a good flight attendant because I care about people and would love the opportunity to take care of your passengers.

- Tell them you only want to work for them.

- Express your desires and let them know how much you want the position!

They may also ask you, <u>Why do you want to work for our company?</u>

- Tell them you would be honored to work for their company and would be proud to wear their wings.

- Let the interviewers know that they are number 1 with you.

- Express your sincere desire to work for them and that you would make an excellent employee.

♦ Be creative in your answers however, remember they are watching how you smile, sit, speak, gesture, laugh, walk, so be careful. If they ask you to relocate to another city, tell them absolutely!

♦ Never hesitate. Don't say well, I'm not sure. Let them know you will go anywhere they ask you.

Let's take a minute and talk about transferring to a new city. Is it for you? *Can you pick up and go just like that? Would you be able to leave your friends and family?* Give the question some thought, could you move away from all your family and friends? It is very difficult! I should know I went through it. You must be committed to this job! It is very important to take it seriously.

When I first got to Salt Lake City, it was exciting living in a new town. I had never lived where it snowed before. The winter came and it got very cold. I then realized how alone I was. My family lived in Los Angeles and I was alone in a big city without friends. Somehow I persevered and got through it by flying home as often as I could. Eventually, I settled down and things were okay.

It's important to think about these things, before you make the choice to become a flight attendant. It's very possible that you could be based away from your family, so look deep inside and see if this is the job for you.

Think of the many challenges of beginning a new life somewhere. You might meet the man or woman of your dreams. I was fortunate to meet my husband in Salt Lake City. If it's meant to be in your life, it will happen to you.

If the interviewers ask you, <u>How would you handle an emergency situation?</u>

41

- ◆ Tell them you would stay calm and in control.

- ◆ You would follow the emergency guidelines and procedures.

- ◆ You would shout your commands and assist the passengers to the exits (they want to know that you won't panic in an emergency situation. Keep in mind that they're looking to see that you are not frightened or timid about emergency situations). Tell them the answer with confidence because that's what they're looking for.

Here's another way they could ask you questions, so be prepared.

The representatives will be in the front of the room at a table. The applicants will sit in a row directly in front of them. The interviewers will go down the line and ask you question's individually. When they ask you the question, smile and speak clearly. Make sure they can hear you. Don't worry about how long it takes you to answer, give a solid and complete answer.

If the representatives put you in a group of six people and ask you to solve a problem, here's what you should do.

The question is <u>How would you handle an irate passenger in first class?</u>

- ◆ Take charge of the group

- ◆ Gather everyone around and discuss the problem.

♦ Listen to the other applicants to hear their ideas.

The representatives will be watching to see who is aggressive and who is passive. They will also be watching to see if you're a group player. The key is to display all of these qualities. Have a little fun, don't appear too serious or too controlling. Show that you can be flexible. Let me give you an example of an irate passenger.

A man was sitting in first class and he had too much to drink. One of the flight attendants noticed him being loud and spilling his drink on himself and the person next to him. When the intoxicated man asked for another drink he blurted out obscene language. "Sir," she replied, "I'm sorry but I believe you've had too much to drink and you're upsetting the other passengers." He got very upset and insisted that she bring him another drink. The flight attendant excused herself and went to get the flight attendant in charge. They both were able to control the situation and insure the safety of the passengers.

If a passenger appears drunk and out of control, the correct thing to do is evaluate the situation and solve the problem. If you feel the situation is out of your control, call the flight attendant in charge. Two heads are better than one! Be very careful what you say to the passengers, you don't want to make matters worse. This is the type of answer the airlines are looking for. Solve the question by saying you would not offer any more drinks. You would find out what the problem was with the passenger and try and solve it. Offer the customer something to calm them down. Apologize to them and offer something complimentary if possible.

What the representatives look for:

When you arrive at the interview be on your best behavior! The representatives will be watching your every move. Go up to the other applicants and introduce yourself. You can bet the representatives are watching to see how you interact with the other applicants. Their eyes will be scanning the room, seeking out those who stand out. No one knows what the representatives are looking for, it could be a certain smile, or personality they're looking for. I once heard that some interviewers hire about twenty to thirty applicants in one interview session with the same characteristics. It just depends on what they're looking for on the day of your interview. Just be yourself and what will be, will be.

After we all gathered in the room the airline representatives introduced themselves. They talked about the company and the interview process. They told us that they would call our names out randomly and we were to walk to the front of the room.

How to present yourself at the group interview:

When your name is called out, stand up and walk to the front of the room. As you walk by the interviewers smile and say hello. If time permits shake their hands. Never walk by the interviewers without some kind of greeting. The interviewers will be watching your every move, so make sure your posture is upright and watch how you walk.

After you greet the representatives, turn around and smile at the applicants. Tell them your name and where you're from. Continue to tell them what you're doing in your life, are you going to school? Or working? After you tell them your name and where you're from, tell them you're honored that they would have you there for the interview. Express to them there is no other place you would rather be.

When you say this, look at the interviewer and smile. Explain to them that you are grateful to be there. Be humble! Be gracious! That's what the interviewers are looking for.

Continue to express why you want to be a flight attendant. Explain that you have worked hard in the customer service field and college to prepare yourself for the flight attendant position. Also, don't forget to tell the interviewers that you will make an excellent employee and will be faithful to their company. After you tell them about your life and how much you want to become a flight attendant, thank the interviewers for having you there and return to your seat.

How I survived my interview process with Delta Airlines:

After all the applicants settled in their seats, the representatives began calling our names out randomly. When they called my name, I smiled and graciously walked down the isle. I walked by the interviewers and simply said Hi! I didn't appear over anxious, or bored. I looked very natural. In fact, I felt as if I was glowing! I then turned to the representatives and said, first of all I am honored that Delta would have me here today. Then I turned to the applicants and told them my name and where I was from. I remember the interviewers were writing notes about me and looked at me with promise in their eyes. I then explained I was attending San Diego State University and working in a department store. Toward the end of the interview, I summed it up by expressing my sincere desire to become a flight attendant, thanked the representatives and returned to my seat.

Later, I was called back to a room with one interviewer where we reviewed my application.

Secrets to the one on one interview:

After the group interview they will call you back for the one on one interview. They will take you back to a room where they will ask you questions. As you walk with the interviewer into the room, wait for them to sit down first. Always be on your best behavior! Introduce yourself with a handshake and wait for the interviewer to initiate the conversation. They will probably go over your application with you first, so make sure you answered every question truthfully. They will go over your school records and work history.

After you have gone over your application, they will ask you again, "Why do you want to be a flight attendant? How would you benefit our company?" The interviewers are trying to see how well you communicate and what kind of personality you have. Create a bond with your interviewer, ask them questions and form a common interest. Find a way to make your interviewer laugh! Everyone enjoys people who can make him or her laugh.

How to get to the physical:

After the one on one interview, you will be directed to another room where you will await the physical. It's been my experience that if you go home from the interview without a physical, you are not hired. If they tell you they'll contact you in a couple of weeks, it's a sure indication that you're not being considered for the job. However, if you're of the lucky one's and you are chosen to attend the physical here's what to expect. The representatives will lead you out the secret door and onto a company van. When you arrive at the building, they will ask you to fill out paperwork. After you have filled out all the forms, Then they will take you to a room where they will test your eye-site, hearing, blood, and you will have to take a drug test. The physical usually lasts all day. Once you have completed the tests, the company will fly you back home and you will receive a letter in the mail telling you when to attend training.

Don't worry you can do this! Just follow what I say and you will see that you too can Follow Your Dreams!

TAMMY CLARK

<u>CHAPTER IV</u>

What to Expect in Training

TAMMY CLARK

Training is very difficult! Pay attention in class and listen closely to your instructors.

The following subjects are normally covered in class:

- CITY CODES
- GENERAL FLIGHT KNOWLEDGE
- PA ANNOUNCEMENTS
- SERVICING TECHNIQUES
- PASSENGER RELATIONS
- PASSENGER SAFETY
- FAA RULES
- SECURITY
- EVACUATIONS
- FIRST AIDE
- WATER EVACUATIONS
- COMPANY HISTORY AND TRADITIONS
- GENERAL PROCEDURES
- BOARDING PROCEDURES
- SERVICE STANDARDS AND PROCEDURES
- CABIN DOORS
- WINDOW EXITS
- GALLEY LOCATIONS
- JUMP SEAT STAFFING
- EMERGENCY EQUIPMENT LOCATION
- COCKPIT

- ✈ UPPER AND LOWER GALLEY OPERATIONS
- ✈ PORTABLE OXYGEN BOTTLES
- ✈ FLASH LIGHT LOCATION AND OPERATION
- ✈ COFFEE AND OVEN OPERATION
- ✈ LIFE VEST
- ✈ RAFT LOCATION
- ✈ LAVATORY SMOKE DETECTORS
- ✈ SERVING STANDARDS
- ✈ FIRE EXTINGUISHER (OPERATION AND LOCATION)
- ✈ PROTECTIVE BREATHING EQUIPMENT
- ✈ FIRST CLASS AND COACH SERVICE
- ✈ EMERGENCY PROCEDURES
- ✈ LAND EVACUATION
- ✈ BELLY LANDING
- ✈ NOSE GEAR COLLAPSE
- ✈ DITCHING PROCEDURES
- ✈ AIRCRAFT FIRE EVACUATION
- ✈ MEDICAL AND FIRST AID KITS

The instructors will provide you with a booklet covering each subject. Let's talk about one of the most important things learned at flight school, **"Emergency Procedures."** You must be able to operate and evacuate through the airplanes (mock up) doors. The doors are very heavy so be careful! You will be asked to shout commands such as, **"Good exit, come this way."** Training is very intense. Study all materials given to you. If you pay attention in class you shouldn't have a problem. It is mandatory that you maintain a 90% grade point average throughout training.

Throughout training you will learn how to evacuate a smoke filled cabin, jump down a slide, put out a fire and escape through window exits. Sound exciting? You can do it!

Examples:

How to put out a lavatory fire:

- Don your facemask
- Aim at the base of the fire
- Spray.

The instructors will grade you on this.

Most training centers have a pool where you learn survival skills. This is where you will learn how to ditch an aircraft, survive in a raft, and learn basic water safety skills. Everyone has to participate in the drills. The instructors will teach you how to evacuate the aircraft and jump in the raft. You can do this! This is good training because you never know what can happen when you're flying. That's why so much time is spent on evacuation procedures.

In class you will receive booklets covering each subject.

City codes review:

ABQ	ALBUQUERQUE, NM
ACA	ACAPULCO, MEX
AGS	AUGUSTA, GA
ALB	ALBANY, NY
AMA	AMARILLO, TX
ANC	ANCHORAGE, AK
ATL	ATLANTA, GA

AUS	AUSTIN, TX
BDA	BERMUDA
BDL	HARTFORD, CT/SPRINGFIELD, MA
BGR	BANGOR, ME
BHM	BIRMINGHAM, AL
BIL	BILLINGS, MT
BIS	BISMARK/MANDAN, ND
BNA	NASHVILLE, TN
BOI	BOISE, ID
BOS	BOSTON, MA
BTM	BUTTE, MT
BTR	BATON ROUGE, LA
BUF	BUFFALO, NY
BUR	BURBANK/HOLLYWOOD, CA
BWI	BALTIMORE, MD
BZN	BOZEMAN, MT
CAE	COLUMBIA, SC
CHA	CHATTANOOGA, TN
CHS	CHARLESTON, SC
CLE	CLEVELAND, OH
CLT	CHARLOTTE, NC
CMH	COLUMBUS, OH
COS	COLORADO SPRINGS, CO
CPR	CASPER, WY
CSG	COLUMBUS, GA
CVG	CINCINNATI, OH
DAB	DAYTONA BEACH, FL
DCA	WASHINGTON, DC (NATIONAL)
DEN	DENVER, CO
DFW	DALLAS/FT. WORTH, TX
DTW	DETROIT, MI
DUB	DUBLIN, IRELAND

ELP	EL PASO, TX
EWR	NEWARK, NJ
FAI	FAIRBANKS, AK
FAT	FRESNO, CA
FCA	KALISPELL, MT
FLL	FT. LAUDERDALE/HOLLYWOOD, FL
FRA	FRANKFURT, GERMANY
FSD	SIOUX FALLS, SD
FWA	FT. WAYNE, IN
GDL	GUADALAJARA, MEX
GEG	SPOKANE, WA
GSO	GREENSBORO/HIGHPOINT/WINSTON-SALEM, NC
GSP	GREENVILLE/SPARTANBURG, SC
GTF	GREAT FALLS, MT
HAM	HAMBURG, GER
HLN	HELENA, MT
HNL	HONOLULU, HI
HOU	HOUSTON, TX
HSV	HUNTSVILLE/DECATUR, AL
IAD	WASHINGTON, DC (DULLES)
IAH	HOUSTON, TX (INTERCONTINENTAL)
ICT	WICHITA, KS
IDA	IDAHO FALLS, ID
IND	INDIANAPOLIS, IN
JAX	JACKSONVILLE, FL
JFK	NEW YORK, NY (KENNEDY INT'L)
JNU	JUNEAU, AK

LAS	LAS VEGAS, NV
LAX	LOS ANGELES, CA
LBB	LUBBOCK, TX
LEX	LEXINGTON, KY
LGA	NEW YORK, NY (LA GUARDIA)
LGB	LONG BEACH, CA
LGW	LONDON, ENGLAND
LIT	LITTLE ROCK, AR
MCI	KANSAS CITY, MO
MCO	ORLANDO, FL
MEM	MEMPHIS, TN
MEX	MEXICO CITY, MEX
MGM	MANTGOMERY, AL
SLC	SALT LAKE CITY, UT
SMF	SACRAMENTO, CA
SNA	ORANGE COUNTY/SANTA ANA, CA
SNN	SHANNON, IRELAND
SRQ	SARASOTA/BRADENTON, FL
STL	ST. LOUIS, MO
STR	STUTTGART, GER
SYR	SYRACUSE, NY
TLH	TALLAHASSEE, FL
TOL	TOLEDO, OH
TPA	TAMPA/ST. PETERSBURG - CLEARWATER, FL
TPE	TAIPEI, TAIWAN
TUL	TULSA, OK
TUS	TUCSON, AZ
TYS	KNOXVILLE, TN
YEG	EDMONTON, ALBERTA, CANADA
YUL	MONTREAL, QUEBEC, CANADA

YVR	VANCOUVER, BRITISH COLUMBIA, CANADA
YYC	CALGARY, ALBERTA, CANADA
ZIH	IXTAPA/ZIHUATANEJO, MEX

CONGRATULATIONS! You have just learned approximately 100 airport codes.

There are certain terms used in the airline industry that are not familiar to the public. In dealing with the passengers you should use the correct terminology. Study and memorize the following terms. You can expect to see them on all of your exams.

Equipment: Another name for aircraft.

Fuselage: The main body of the airplane.

Bulkhead: Wall separating cabins on an aircraft.

Captain's Side: Left side of aircraft.

First Officer's Side: Right side of aircraft.

Jumpseat: Flight attendant seat on the airplane.

Galley: Kitchen area.

Flight Attendant Panel: Located adjacent to flight attendant seat.

Line of Time: A flight attendant's schedule for the month.

Bid: Each month flight attendant's bid for a schedule.

Seniority Number: All flight attendants are assigned a system seniority number.

Load Factor: Extra flight attendant.

Deadhead: A pilot or flight attendant who is scheduled to fly as a non-working crew member going to or returning from working a trip.

Reserve: A flight attendant who is on-call as a back up to cover trips when senior flight attendant's call in sick.

FAIC: Flight Attendant In Charge. Another name is A-line.

Emergency Equipment: Pieces of equipment that are used for aircraft emergencies.

IFSC: In Flight Service Coordinator.

Equipment Change: Changing from one airplane to another.

Turnaround: A trip that begins at your base and returns there without a designated off-duty rest period in another city.

FAA: The Federal Aviation Administration.

Recurrent Training: The FAA requires that Flight Attendants pass recurrent training every year.

Cockpit: Where the pilots fly the aircraft.

Re-route: A change in routing of a scheduled trip.

Now that I have taken you through the business aspects of training, let me share with you my experience.

The day I received my letter informing me that I was going to flight school was one of the happiest days of my life. I was going to Atlanta to attend 4 weeks of training. I received my free pass in the mail from Delta and was on my way. Even though this was a dream come true, I was very nervous about training. I didn't know what to expect. That's why I want to share it with you so you have some idea before you go.

When I got to Atlanta, I couldn't believe how big the airport was. I finally made it outside where the taxicabs were and went directly to the training center across the street from the airport. When I arrived at the training center, I met up with some other trainees and we all walked up to the front lobby. The lady at the desk signed us in and gave us room numbers. I was so excited to be there, I felt like I was in heaven. This was my dream come true!

I went to my room and looked around. I went to the window, where I could see the jets landing and taking off. I was in my glory!

Suddenly, the door opened and my roommate entered. We said hello to each other then she asked me what side of the room I wanted, "My things are already by the window, I replied, so I'll take that side." I finished putting my things away and went out to the lobby to meet the other trainees. I then went on my own private tour of the training center and to meet the new trainees in the lobby.

TAMMY CLARK

Soon the day ended and we were settling in for a good night sleep. The next morning we got up at 7:30 a.m. to be in the auditorium at 8:a.m., sharp. I couldn't believe it, to my surprise people were running into the auditorium late. If you get caught coming in late too many times you can get kicked out of the training center! Never, be late. Especially in training, they won't tolerate it. I was always ten to fifteen minutes early I was too paranoid to be any later. I took it very seriously.

I remember sitting there waiting for the pep rally to start which welcomes in the new trainees. I had tears in my eyes. I couldn't believe my dream was here. I was sitting right in the midst of everything I had waited for all my life. Finally, the rally started and the teachers introduced themselves along with management. It was great! I felt very welcome. After the rally, we went directly to our classrooms and were assigned seats. There were two people to every desk and the instructors were in the front of the classroom. Our first test was on city codes. Don't forget to memorize city codes! You can bet it will be on your first test and the instructors will expect you to get 100%. It is very important to impress your instructors early because you never know when you might need their help later on.

That's why it is important to keep a professional image with everyone. Don't get caught up in clicks and people who would rather party than study.

There were a couple of people in my class that almost got kicked out for too much partying. So beware! I don't understand how these people can go out and get trashed then show up for class expected to maintain a 90% grade point average. I didn't have time to party, I was too busy studying.

The second day the instructors took us down to the basement where the mockup airplanes were. It was quite intimidating! We toured around the building then went back to the classroom and prepared for another test. Every day we had a test on something. As the days passed we learned how to open and close airplane doors, evacuate, and assist people down the slide.

After a couple of weeks we were heavily into evacuation drills and emergency procedures. The instructors told us to sit in the passenger seats inside the mock-up airplane and prepare to be called to play flight attendant in charge. I was terrified to get up in front of everyone and do something I had never done before. Unfortunately, they found me in the back of the airplane where I was hiding and told me to sit in the jump seat. I put my hands under my legs for take off and then the instructor played the music of a crash. I began shouting the commands, "Grab your ankles, Heads down, Stay low!" I then unfastened my seat belt and called the cockpit.

The captain told me to evacuate, so I started shouting, "Release your seat belts." At the same time I opened the door and shouted, "Good exit, come this way."

Everyone jumped down the slide. The instructors will grade you on this so you don't want to fail. They will make you do it over and over until you get it right.

We then went to the poolroom where the mock-up plane was. We changed into our bathing suits and jumped into the pool with our life vest on. We all practiced water safety and learned how to float. After this it was time to learn how to evacuate the airplane and get into the rafts. So we went back into the dressing rooms and changed out of our swimsuits.

We all gathered inside the airplane and the instructors told us where to sit. They told us we were going to practice ditching the airplane. The instructors randomly selected people to play flight attendant. Thank God I wasn't one of them. I was so nervous! I felt it would have been better just watching! Anyway, the instructors played the audio of a crash, then suddenly it stopped and all the emergency lights came on. The flight attendants opened the doors and shouted their commands, "Good exit, come this way!"

We all evacuated through the doors and into the rafts. After everyone was in the rafts we cut the mooring line that's attached to the airplane. We learned how to survive in the raft. The instructors showed us how to set up a canopy for protection and how to use a flair gun. We spent so much time on drills and evacuations, it's so important. You have to know what you're doing that's why they put you through a vigorous training course.

As the weeks went on we learned about FAA rules and what to expect on board the aircraft. We went through everything! Training was hard for me, I felt like I was failing the whole time.

By the third week, we were still having tests every day and we went on several field trips. The field trips were fun! We went to the Delta hanger where we boarded an L10-11. It was a monster! I had never seen an airplane so big! The inside completely intimidated me. I thought to myself, "How in the world am I going to work this thing?" I thought I would never pass the training flight we were assigned at the end of training. With a little prayer I managed to get through it.

It was pretty amusing flying for the first time as a flight attendant trainee. We had no idea what the heck we were doing. We were just observing the other flight attendants doing their job and really, just getting in the way. Everything seemed like a blur, it all happened so fast! From Atlanta to Orlando we had 50 minutes to do a beverage service. I remember seeing the cart go up the plane then down the plane so fast my head was spinning! These flight attendants were working so fast that I couldn't keep up. I had to laugh the entire time. It was so funny! Everyone was running around the airplane trying to get the service done, looking like a bunch of chickens with our heads cut off! Even the passengers were looking at us like we were crazy.

It was nice toward the end of the flight talking to the passengers and feeling like a real flight attendant. I finally got back to Atlanta and headed back to the training center, where I settled in for the night.

The next morning, I got up and prepared for a test. The days were getting shorter now and we were approaching graduation. Finally, the day I had been waiting for!

I was now preparing for finals. I was struggling to keep 90% average all the way through, I had to study hard. If you're really committed, you can do this. I had to buckle down and concentrate on what I was doing in training.

I'll never forget the day my instructor told me I passed the finals and I was a full fledge flight attendant! It was like no other feeling I had ever experienced before. I jumped in her arms and hugged her! I was so happy! I ran out of the room and called my parents to let them know.

I could hardly sleep that night because I was filled with excitement. As I lay there dreaming about graduation day, I drifted off to sleep. It seemed I had just shut my eyes when the morning light filled the room and my eyes. I awoke with a smile on my face and joy in my heart. I was on my way to my dream. I remember the moment I put on my uniform and looked in the mirror. I never knew I could feel so much joy!

As I slipped on my navy blue suit and navy blue stockings, I could feel the fire of doing what you're meant to do in life. I was fulfilling a dream. It was very emotional for me to look in the mirror and see myself in uniform. I felt a sense of pride and responsibility. It gave me self-esteem.

I hope you can experience the same feeling I did. It's the best feeling in the world to stand there with your classmates to receive your wings of gold! If you pay attention in class and do your homework, you can get through training. Listen to your instructors in class. They will tell you what's on the test.

Don't worry about the little things, concentrate on keeping a good record at all times. **Follow Your Dreams!**

CHAPTER V

What to Expect On the Job

TAMMY CLARK

Your first day will be very hectic, however if you follow my suggestions and tips, you will know what to expect.

Get to work early, at least twenty minutes before check in. This way you will be able to take care of business in the flight lounge. I always gave myself at least a half an hour to work on the computer, receive e-mail, call scheduling and trade trips.

After you're finished with the little details, you'll meet with the other flight attendants on your trip. I can't stress this enough, get along with the other flight attendants, make friends; it will pay of in the end! What do I mean by this? Well, you never know who might be your next supervisor. It can be very difficult getting along with everyone but it's very important to do.

There are many personalities among flight attendants, and I found it very difficult to deal with all of them. Getting to know someone new on each flight, coexisting with them for three days in a small airplane, let alone a small galley. This can turn into a valuable lesson if you pay attention. Learning to deal with a wide variety of people will make you well rounded in the end. It is definitely a mental challenge trying to learn new things on your first day as well as different personalities.

I remember my first flight from Salt Lake City to Seattle. One of the flight attendants got upset with me because she thought I was being slow on the cart. Of course I wasn't being slow, I was enjoying the passengers and trying to figure out how to work the cart.

There was plenty of time to serve everyone. I think she just wanted to get the service over with. I made the mistake of telling a senior mama (senior flight attendant) to relax while we were on the beverage cart. She got real defensive with me. Later in the galley, I asked her if everything was all right. It was obvious to me she was upset.

I was never really sure why something as little as that would be so upsetting to a senior mama. After all, they should know it's difficult to get the hang of things in the beginning. There will be some flight attendants who care more about sitting in the back of the airplane with a magazine, than they are making the passengers happy. Sometimes I found the passengers easier to deal with than my co-workers! The passengers can be wonderful just remember that you're dealing with a wide variety of people and personalities. It's possible to have bad encounters as well as good ones.

Here's an example of a bad encounter: I was working first class and there was a passenger sitting in 1-C (just in front of my husband). She made a big to do about how I was giving too much attention to the gentleman behind her, my husband. She hassled me the entire flight and made me feel so uncomfortable.

She actually asked to speak to the flight attendant in charge. I couldn't believe that she chose me to pick on. I never did anything to her, I treated her like all the rest of the passengers. I provided her with the drinks she wanted, I checked on her frequently. I don't think passengers have the right to hassle flight attendants because they engage in conversations with other passengers. That's what happens when passengers have too much to drink, as in my situation. Because she decided to cause problems over nothing, I had to document the problem on the flight report. I was actually surprised at her comment about me. Honestly I was always too paranoid to do anything wrong and I don't remember doing anything out of the ordinary. These are the types of situations you will have to deal with. Just do the best you can. Don't let it affect you, move forward and learn from it.

I wanted you to see what really goes on and point out the positives with the negatives. I would like to give you a positive story as well. I can remember a flight that I had that was so special to me.

There was a little old man that was wondering around on the airplane after we de-plained and I asked him if he needed help? "Yes, I'm confused on where to go." He replied. I realized he needed assistance with getting to his connection. I walked him up the jet-way and turned him over to the gate agents. They called for an airport cart to pick him up at the gate. He was so happy that I stayed with him until he was secure and knew what he was doing. That incident touched my heart. If you can take the bad with the good, it will make the job a lot more enjoyable, you'll see! Don't expect to get everything all at once. It takes years to become confident in your position as a flight attendant.

Oh the joy of it all! It's a wonderful career. There are so many things to tell you about the job. I can remember having the party of my life on some of my layovers. Meeting all the crew down in the hotel bar for a few drinks and dancing the night away. By the end of the night we all felt like a bunch of old worn down workhorses dragging ourselves up to bed. Sometimes you really feel like that after a long twelve-hour day.

Layovers can also be a time of loneliness in contrast to the above statement. It can make you think about home a lot and miss family members (take my word for it). It can be brutal if you let it. Honestly you get use to it, so don't fret. The best thing to do is relax on your layover. Take a bath or hot shower and enjoy!

Be very careful on your layover and watch yourself around strangers. There have been incidents in the past regarding safety problems among flight attendants. There have been reports of flight attendants allowing impostors (posing as hotel employees looking to gain access into your room) who are only looking to prey on beautiful young ladies alone in the big city. So please be careful! I'm sure you'll go over safety issues at training. Use common sense and you will do fine. No doubt about it, the flight attendants position is a lot more complex than people think. Some think you're just a waitress in the sky. If they only knew!

Well onto another subject just as interesting, is flying safe? I'm here to say that after six years of flying I never had a major accident. I'll have to admit there were many scary moments but I always felt confident our pilots would see us through. You will have various incidents occur while flying and the key is to know how to handle them with confidence. That's why you carry around a big red book (your flight attendant manual) full of safety procedures. By using the red book you can handle anything that might come your way on board the aircraft. You must carry the red book with you when you fly. It's designed for immediate access to emergency procedure and is a FAA regulation.

You are sent monthly updates and deletions for your red book. Unexpectedly the FAA will come on board and check your red book to see if you've kept it up to date. It's also possible they could ask you specific questions about the airplane.

There will be incidents involving weather, like the time we flew into New Mexico. It was so windy that I thought we were going to land sideways on the runway because of the strong crosswinds that were throwing us around. Even though it seemed scary at the time I was never really afraid, somehow I knew we would make it. Call it faith, confidence in our pilots or just being trained so well. It all comes into play and you react accordingly.

Trying to land in a thunderstorm isn't my idea of fun, but that's exactly what happens quite often.

I remember one time flying into Atlanta, Ga. We hit extreme turbulence on final approach and things started flying everywhere. The coffeepot fell to the floor and things were flying out of the cabinets regardless if they were locked. Just remember to stay calm! Otherwise you could have a panic on your hands. If this should happen to you, don't fret, the pilots will make an announcement regarding weather conditions. In this instance we had to stop preparing the cabin for landing and grab our jumpseats.

Let me walk you through a typical trip.

The day of your trip you should check in early. There is always something to do in the flight lounge.

- ✈ Call scheduling and check in.
- ✈ Check your mailbox.
- ✈ Check your e-mail.
- ✈ Read the mandatory red book.
- ✈ Read all bulletins.
- ✈ Pull up trip on the computer.
- ✈ Attend flight briefing.
- ✈ Greet the airplane.

The flight lounge is where you prepare for your trip and take care of business. Once you have signed in you will meet your crew in the briefing room. The briefing room is where you will discuss the trip. The flight attendant in charge will go over things like; how many people are expected to be on the flight, special meals, movie and liquor sales, kids traveling onboard and special assistance passengers. Everyone will sign up by seniority where they want to sit on the airplane.

After the briefing it will be time to meet the airplane. Make sure you check your mailbox a second time, before you go up to greet the airplane. It's possible a supervisor might have put new mail in your box while you were in the briefing room.

When you get to the airplane the pilots will be doing their pre-flight check. The captain will hold a briefing in first class. Pay close attention to what the captain says, he or she will brief you on the flight. The captain will go over such things as, emergency procedures, weather and flight time. After discussing the business aspect of the flight, everyone may start talking about the layover plans.

This is your chance to make friends with everyone. The layovers can be so much fun. Everyone will usually chat for a while providing there's time, then go to their assigned areas.

The gate agent will come down the jet-way and get someone to board. Now that boarding is taking place, it's time to prepare the cabin. Make sure the cabin is clean and pillows and blankets are picked up. Go through the cabin prior to boarding to check and make sure everything is where it should be. Usually, one person will stay in the cabin to help with luggage and any problems that may arise.

There will be another flight attendant in the back galley preparing the beverage cart and meals. You need to count all of your meals prior to leaving to make sure you have enough. Believe me, you don't want to run out of food on a flight. It's a sure way to make passengers upset and unable to enjoy their flight. It's possible you could get a letter regarding an unhappy customer. If your meals are short, call the flight attendant in charge. This way catering will have time to come back and give you the meals you need. That's why teamwork is so important in this job.

Prepare your beverage cart:

Make sure you have plenty of beer and wine for the flight. I suggest you fill your bins up with ice and plenty of Coke and Diet Coke since those are the most popular drinks. Check to see if your fellow crewmember needs help in the cabin. After everyone has settled into his or her seats, the flight attendant in charge will make a final announcement.

After the gate agent closes the door, the flight attendant will say, "Flight attendants, prepare for departure."

Now arm your doors. Shut the door and put the handle in the armed position. Cross check with the other door to make sure they're both armed and that the girt bar is up. Pick up your phone and do all call. All call is informing the flight attendant in charge that you're armed and crossed checked.

You will then walk through the cabin one last time to make sure everyone has their seat belts on. After completing the safety check, after push back, it's time to lock the galley up for take off. Make a final check of the airplane, then strap your self in the jump seat. Now you can get to know your co-worker and establish a relationship.

This is a good time to get to know the personality of the person you're flying with. Everyone has their own style of working and that's fine, as long as the job gets done. I've worked with some crusty old flight attendants that wouldn't change for anyone. This is when it can get difficult, flying with senior mama's who will most likely tell you what to do. My advice is do what they tell you, providing it's within company rules. Let's admit it, they do have the experience. Don't try and change them, get along with them. It will make you a better flight attendant.

Now I'm not saying you won't come up against some impossible flight attendants to work with, you will. Some can be down right mean, or at least they act that way. If they seem like they don't want to talk much, don't push it. They might be going through something you know nothing about. Do your job and you should be all right.

After take off you should get up and start preparing the beverage cart. Usually two people will work the beverage cart and one person will work the meal cart. Pull the carts to the front of the airplane and begin your service.

Ask the passenger what they would like to drink? If a passenger tells you they want a Coke for example, don't say, "Coke?" Don't repeat yourself unless you didn't hear them. Imagine repeating Coke or Diet Coke all the way down the isle.

I remember a flight attendant that repeated herself over and over again. It sounded awful! The best thing to do is smile and get what they want. Always be courteous and keep a smile on your face. This will reassure the passengers that all is well. The passengers can tell if a crew is not happy and not working well together. Be careful! You might get a letter saying, everyone on the crew looked unhappy and never smiled. You would be surprised what passengers write in about. Do your part and if that should happen, explain to your supervisor.

After the service, you need to pick up all the trays. You will do the relay method most likely. This is where one flight attendant hands the trays to the one in the galley. That person puts them into the catering bins. Don't forget to pick up your pilot's trays in the cockpit. Usually the first class flight attendant takes care of the pilots. If you're in the back you shouldn't worry about it, unless you're told otherwise.

After everything is done you can draw the curtains and have some free time. This is when you can eat what's left over and do personal things. Always remember the passenger comes first, so check on them frequently in the cabin. This is also a good time to get to know some of the passengers.

Walk around the airplane and introduce yourself. Ask the passengers if they would like anything. Socialize with the passengers. You can also go visit the pilots in the cockpit. They get lonely sometimes and would appreciate the visit. Get to know the pilots, they're great! Truthfully they're very fun to be around.

Finally, you arrive at your destination and it's time to prepare the cabin for landing. Pick up everything throughout the cabin. Make sure seat belts are fastened. Secure everything in the galley such as, the coffeepot, meal cart, beverage cart, and cabinets.

Strap yourself in your jump seat and put your hands under your legs for landing. Once you have landed, the flight attendant in charge will say an announcement. When you get to the gate the FAIC will say, "Flight attendants prepare for arrival." Then you disarm your door and cross check.

Make sure the brackets on the girt bar are flush with the floor. This will indicate you're disarmed. Pick up the phone and do all call with the flight attendant in charge. Congratulations! You just completed one leg of a three-day trip.

Usually a 3-day trip will have three legs the first day and four the next. So you can see how much work is involved. It can get very tiring. Keep yourself healthy! You can do this!

I hope this section helped you understand what can happen when you're flying and the many situations that may occur. Flight training will help you become more confident in yourself so that you will know how to handle all emergency situations.

CHAPTER VI

Pros and Cons

TAMMY CLARK

Pros

There are so many wonderful things about the job. Imagine flying above the beautiful snow capped mountains of Colorado, to the cumulus clouds hovering over Miami Beach in one day! This job is so exciting! I knew early in my life that this was the job for me. My heart would not let me give up my dream of becoming a flight attendant. I knew it would be the greatest experience of my life.

Be prepared to literally take off in a whole new direction. It's the beginning of many wonderful things to come. I was on such a high when that happened to me. You must remember how long it took me to get hired. It was eight long years before I was hired by Delta Airlines.

I'm proud to say that I was a Delta flight attendant, in my opinion they are the best of the best. Delta Airlines had the best flight attendant training in my eyes. I hope when you are hired that you discover what I did, and fulfill your dreams as well.

There are so many things I learned while I was on the job. It gave me confidence, responsibility, self-assurance, and a unique opportunity to see the world. Being apart of a big company gave me the self-esteem I was looking for and the ability to grow as a person because of the unique experiences that I went through.

Every year you will attend a unique experience called, Jet Recurrent. Seriously, it is a unique experience. This is where you will rebuild your confidence and refresh your memory on emergency procedures. You must pass the test with a 90% grade point average. If you fail the test they will make you take it over and if you fail again, your supervisor will be notified. You do not want this to happen because you will have to take the test in your supervisor's office. The FAA requires that you pass Jet Recurrent to re-qualify as a flight attendant. If you fail all the attempts to pass the test, you have to go back to training for one week.

It is also recorded in your file. I was fortunate to have maintained a good file while I was flying. Incidents will happen regardless of how many years you've been flying. This all plays a part in how successful you are as a flight attendant.

The best times are when the entire crew gets along. Like the trip I had to Hawaii. After we all checked into the hotel, we met downstairs at the restaurant where we ate and drank until we were sick! The wonderful thing about it is how you bond with your fellow crewmembers. It's something you will never forget. The friendship that is between you will always be a fond memory. There are so many fond memories that I would like to share with you, and hope one day you can experience them as well.

Let's talk free passes! The greatest thing about the passes is being able to take your family on free trips! Depending on what airline you're working for, you are able to take your parents on two free passes a year and your husband flies stand by at any time.

When I first told my parents about the free passes, they said, "Oh how nice." They had no idea the fortune they had just stumbled upon. I mean this was like hitting the lottery. It took some convincing for them to wake up and smell the coffee. They were not travelers! I tried to convince them to take a trip, but they seemed uninterested. Finally, I had to resort to trickery! Seriously, they would not budge.

I remember, one day I told them they had better use their passes before I get married or they wouldn't be able to use them anymore. So I made them a deal. I told my dad I wanted him to go to Hawaii for his vacation and that I was going to go with them. He finally said yes! I can't even begin to tell you how it changed my dad's life. He actually returned a different man. It reminded me of Moses going to the mountain and having a life changing experience. Today believe it or not you can find him in his backyard in California with his Hawaiian beads on, basking in the sun. It's the truth! And on a really good day, he'll have his Hawaiian music on. They were so impressed with the whole experience that they went several more times.

As you can see there are many wonderful events ready to take place in your life. This job will truly change your life! So take it all in and ENJOY!

Cons

I don't want to discourage you but it's important to know what goes on behind closed doors. Let me share with you what I observed throughout my six years of flying.

Personally, I found some of the trips to be horrible! Early sign in times, and late flight hours were impossible! Believe it or not the flight attendants had a special name for one of those trips, "The trip from hell." Of course when I was on reserve it was the only trip I got. Flight attendants were so desperate to get off the trip, they would call in sick, suddenly hurt themselves, or be lucky enough to trade off the trip. Sign in for this trip was 4:50 a.m., not to mention this terrible trip arrived at the layover destination at 11:00p.m. It had a long layover, however you slept most of the day. I always wondered why scheduling never changed the format of the trip so it would be easier to fly and not as many flight hours. I hope conditions have changed for the future generations of flight attendants.

Another issue that bothered me was the lack of warm clothing we were allowed to wear. Everything you wear has to be approved by your supervisor. I remember being so cold that it actually affected my health. I was sick all the time. I was only allowed to wear a white blouse under my jacket or sweater with my suit. We were not permitted to where heavy jackets on board unless the passengers wear off the airplane. I'm just simply trying to say that we should have had a better selection of warm attire to choose from for those cold trips. Even the jacket that was approved for us to wear wasn't warm enough. Hopefully that has all changed by now.

If you like confusion and irregular hours this is the job for you! Oh, and don't forget you have to like people. What I mean by confusion and irregular hours is you have to be flexible. This job is tough! Take a flight and see for yourself how much the flight attendants work.

It's common to see a trip sign in late and get in the next morning. When I was flying it was called an all nighter. Consider all the time zones you go through, from coast to coast. I can't stress enough that you try and eat as healthy as you can. It's difficult because you don't have a set schedule when you're flying. I suggest bringing nutrition bars or fruits and vegetables with you when you fly. It's very uncomfortable when you're tired and cold on the airplane so dress as warm as you can and stay healthy.

One of the things I observed within the flight attendant group was the lack of camaraderie. I remember many times flight attendants telling on each other like little kids, it was crazy.

I had a bizarre incident happen to me on one of my trips. Scheduling had assigned me flight attendant in charge, on a trip to Houston. When I arrived at the plane to fulfill my duties, there were two other flight attendants there who greeted me, as I boarded the aircraft. One of the girls said, "I want to fly A-line on the way back to Houston." (A-line means flight attendant in charge.) I explained scheduling had assigned me A-line and I was getting paid for it. She continued to insist she was going to work as A-line on the return trip I finally said, "We can call scheduling and see what they have to say about it." She finally backed down and went to the back of the airplane. Later in the flight they were rude to me and barely talked to me. This is what I mean when I talk about camaraderie. After the service was completed and we were preparing for initial approach they came up to first class where I was and struck up a conversation with me. We all apologized to each other for the miss-communication we had. After we landed in Houston and all the passengers were off the plane, they came up from the back with their luggage and said the ritual, "Well, nice flying with you and hope you have a good flight home." Being the A-line, I had to turn in the liquor money in Houston before I returned to Salt Lake City. So, one of the girls offered to turn it in for me. I told her sure, and thanked her. At that moment I was happy everything turned out well between us and there were no major problems.

The next day, I received a phone call from my supervisor. To my surprise those sweet Delta flight attendants had written me up! They claimed that I was difficult! They also claimed that I would not allow them to work A-line. I was just doing my job and fulfilling my responsibilities. After all, scheduling assigned me the position and I was getting paid for it. They were the ones who caused all the problems in the first place. After I explained it to my supervisor she looked up the information in the computer and verified the information that I had provided was correct. She agreed with me and stated I was in the right. The other girls really had no business making a fuss and they appeared to be the difficult ones.

My supervisor ripped up the letter and tossed it in the trash. It never went on my record. I wrote a letter about them and as far as I know, it's still in their records! I never saw them again. Thank God (back stabbers!) I'm just telling it like it is. That's why you need to take the bad with the good and try to do the best job you can. At the time this all happened it seemed like there was a lot of complaining going on within the flight attendant group. Expect ups and downs within the company you fly with.

I wanted to be a part of the Delta family as it use to be, before the big buy out of Pan Am. Unfortunately, the company grew so big that we lost the close family feeling we all had between the years of 1990-1993. The flight attendant group was much larger and in my opinion never got back that good ol' southern family we use to be.

After 6 years of flying I decided that I no longer had the desire to fly and had fulfilled everything I had dreamed about as a flight attendant. I was ready to move on in my life. I realized that I had changed and had other desires I wanted to fulfill in my life like staying home, seriously. After flying for six years I wanted to just sit at home and do nothing!

This job is not for everyone. That's why I'm trying to give you a perspective. I remember a girl in training that quit before her six-month probationary period was up. She was so homesick for Tennessee. Sometimes a job may appear to be something it's really not.

When you first get hired with the airlines they will put you on reserve. Reserve flight attendants cover trips for sick line holders, or if there are any open trips in the system. I was on reserves for six months and it was a difficult place to be. You feel like you have no social life. When you're on reserve, scheduling can call you out any time, day or night but they must give you at least one hour to get to the airport.

I kept one bag packed so I was ready to go at anytime. I hated getting the bad trips that line holders swapped off for. It was terrible getting the same trip over and over.

I really want you to get a feel for what the job is really like. That is why I'm giving you these examples of what to expect. Keep in mind this job is mentally and physically exhausting. If you don't have stamina, it's not the job for you.

Lessons to be learned at layovers.

I went on a trip to Honolulu where we stayed at the Hilton. The trip was exhausting, and by the time we got to the hotel all we could do was sleep. The layover was twenty-four hours long, which was nice. It's just that on the flight back home to Salt Lake City, we had to fly an all-nighter. One of the flight attendants told me the best way to survive the all-nighter was to get up very early the next morning and take a nap in the afternoon. Wrong! I couldn't go to sleep. The sound of waves crashing on the beach exhilarated me. I wanted to be out in the sun, not sleeping in the hotel room mid-afternoon. Unfortunately, I ended up staying awake for twenty-four hours. When we got to Salt Lake City, I was holding my stomach trying not to get sick. I would have been better off if I would have stayed up the night we got in and slept in the next morning. Now you know what to do! Enjoy Hawaii!

I believe the job is up to you, and how you're able to deal with each and every situation as a whole. If you're not totally committed to the job, you won't last long. I say "Go for it and experience it for yourselves."

<u>CHAPTER VII</u>

Behind Closed Doors

TAMMY CLARK

There are many hidden secrets within the airline industry that are rarely seen by the public. Do you ever wonder what goes on behind closed doors? Well you're about to find out!

You know what it's like to walk on egg shells right? That's what it felt like everyday I went to work. I don't know where it originated but within the company there was a constant fear of being "written up." Why the company allowed this is beyond me. It created a sense of paranoia, especially within the flight attendant group. Management made it clear that getting a negative letter from passengers or co-workers could jeopardize your career. It's very difficult to prove your innocence once a letter is written about you.

Management always takes the side of the passengers for fear of loosing them as customers. This puts a lot of pressure on employees who are trying to do the best job they can. Nevertheless, the fear of saying the wrong thing or making a mistake causes most employees to back away from passenger problems. I witnessed this on several occasions. Flight attendants didn't want to get involved for fear they would receive a negative letter. They would rather avoid passenger problems than receive a letter that stays in their file for the rest of their career. Do you blame them? Of course not, they want to protect their jobs. Bad things are going to happen! I don't believe that every negative letter that comes from a passenger should stay in your file for the rest of your career. When you're dealing with hundreds of passengers, it's inevitable that something is going to go wrong, why should a letter determine your role as a flight attendant? Negative letters should go in a separate file under things that go wrong.

They shouldn't target flight attendants, who in most cases can't control every situation that comes up. We are trained to deal with all situations. When things go wrong and you're involved, there shouldn't be a choice between getting involved and getting a negative letter. Some passengers just want to complain and management should stand behind their employees under these circumstances, not just throw the letter in your file and say, "Sorry."

Okay, now that I have defended all the flight attendants of the world, lets talk about the ones who are cranky, moody, cold and tired! You will have to find a way to get along with them because they have been around for a long time and they don't want any crap from the new kids on the block! There's a stigma within the group that if you're not at least six years seniority, you're considered a junior. The senior mama's love to remind you of this in so many ways. It's funny, once you reach a certain level in seniority, the senior mama's treat you much better.

There's another reason why flight attendants are cranky and irritable most of the time, it's the long hours. For instance, scheduling assigns you a trip called the Stand Up. You sign in at eight thirty p.m. and do one leg to your layover, get up the next morning, do one leg home after only getting a couple hours of sleep. This schedule is three days on, and three days off. After you do this for a month, it takes a toll on you.

Even though it's tough to work, the senior mama's will not trade off. You can see my point, this kind of schedule can make you crazy due to lack of sleep, and the inability to keep a normal schedule.

Let me tell you another secret about flight attendants that will surprise you! If you don't know how to cut lemons and limes, let the senior mama do it. I got chewed out one time because I cut the limes wrong. Apparently they didn't hang correctly on the glass. I'm thinking, **excuse me!** You know what

I mean? They don't tell you that in training! I had to laugh when she scolded me. Okay, you know I'm going to teach you the correct way to cut lemons and limes, the flight attendant way!

Here's the secret:

Cut the ends off the lemon or lime. Cut the lemon down the center to make two halves. Make a slit across each side of the lemon, then cut into pieces. Hang the lemon on the rim of the glass. Never make round circles or other shapes when serving passengers. Practice cutting the lemons and limes at home before you go to training!

In training, they will teach you how to make up a caddy. You put things in it like, tea bags, stir sticks, lemons, limes, aspirin and napkins. The caddy goes on top of the beverage cart. The training center will have a mock up aircraft for you to practice. Remember you're flying with seasoned flight attendants that have been flying for years. They know most of the time what works and what doesn't, so follow their lead. The key is for everyone to work together in harmony because if you don't, your trip could be a disaster!

It is so important that you know what you're doing as a flight attendant. There is a lot of responsibility in this job. I've seen what can happen when the crew doesn't click.

I was on this trip from Salt Lake City to Atlanta on the L-1011 and the crew didn't click from the beginning. You could feel it from the moment at sign in, until we got to the briefing room. Flight attendants not getting along etc... you catch my drift, right! Well by the time we got to the airplane the gossip already started about someone doing something wrong or maybe they just had a communication breakdown! Anyway, their attitudes created a problem during the meal service. They were fighting and carrying on and we almost didn't finish our service.

Unfortunately, this happens quite often. I don't know why. Maybe it's the nature of the business. Long hours, short layovers, working in a small environment with to many co-workers, lack of sleep, time zones, passenger stress, G-force stress, temperature change, climate change, etc ... there's a lot of things people don't think about when they think of a flight attendant.

If you see your crew is lacking camaraderie, and is struggling with the service, don't be surprised if you get a negative letter from a non-rev. Watch your back! Find out where they are on the airplane, their names will be listed on the departure report. They are very capable of writing you up behind your back even if you think you did a good job! Follow the rules and you shouldn't see too many letters in your file. I have seen it happen where a non-rev was traveling and had a tiff with one of the flight attendants over something and it got out of control. When we got to our destination, they all went out to the gate area to hash it out. The captain and copilot were there because the non- rev was a pilot also. It made it all the way down to the supervisor's office. Don't assume everything is going perfect. Believe me, you'll know if you deserve it or not. You can certainly dispute it, if you know it's not true. The majority of the time the trips are fine.

When I first started flying, I had an incident with a gate agent. I had just arrived from Hawaii to Los Angeles and was assigned to "deadhead" back to my base in Salt Lake City. I went up to the desk to check in with the gate agent and as I handed him my ticket, I asked him if he thought I could get on the flight. He ignored me! I asked him again and he snapped at me. I was so embarrassed that I whispered to him, "What is the problem?" He continued to act rude towards me and handed me my ticket. I was so upset that I called his supervisor on the phone and told her that he gave me a hard time. I told her I was just trying to get home on the next flight. She came down to where we were and spoke to both of us. She told us that we had to write a letter about what happened and our supervisors would talk to us about the incident later.

As I said earlier, not every situation needs a letter of explanation that stays in your file! These unforeseen communication breakdowns are bound to happen. I found out later that he was totally stressed out and took it out on me. He knew I was on my six month probationary period. Give me a break! One thing I learned, is that even though it might not be your fault, sometimes it's better not to get a supervisor involved. Getting a supervisor involved means a letter in your file. It's kind of a double edge sword, do you take the abuse? Or call a supervisor and get a letter in your file? Even if it's not your fault and your motivation is documenting the incident, it doesn't matter it still goes in your file and creates a negative record.

If you complain too much about your co-worker, it can reflect back on you and your supervisor will be asking you questions. Personally, I let a lot of incidents go for fear of getting too many letters in my file. I avoided situations that would cause me to have a flawed record.

My advice is do the best you can and the passengers and co-workers will reward you with good letters. Believe me, your co-workers will notice if you're doing a good job or not. I was lucky to have received many good letters while I was flying. In this business, reputation is everything.

Now let's talk about calling in sick to scheduling. Be prepared, they have a way of making you feel guilty. They will say things like, "Are you sure you can't make it in," or "We are short on reserves, it's going to be hard to fill your position." Here's the icing on the cake! They expect you to be illness free your first six months. That's like setting you up for failure. When you enter into a new environment, the potential to get sick is always there. Especially when you're flying with sick people, you can't get away from them. Unfortunately, you're stuck breathing all the germs that float around inside the airplane.

Circulation throughout the main cabin is poor, there's hardly any fresh air. You would think they would consider these things and allow you to call in sick at least once during your first six months. I'll admit it I got sick my first six months and they called me into the office about it.

Let me tell you about the time I got sick and was forced to fly. The morning of my trip, I woke up at 4:30 a.m. and was sick to my stomach. I went to the kitchen and made some coffee, in hopes that it might help my stomach. I drank a glass of juice, but I still felt the same. I decided at that point to call scheduling and inform them that I had the flu. After I explained my situation to the lady in scheduling, to my surprise she told me that if I didn't show up for work, she would give me a no-show on my record. It didn't matter to her that I woke up with the flu and couldn't work, she was more concerned about filling my position with a reserve than she was about my health.

Toward the end of the conversation, she told me that I could talk to my supervisor about the no-show, but that she couldn't be sure it would be taken off my record, so I made the decision to go to work. Big mistake! It really hit me when I got to work. It was so early, that when I got to the flight attendant lounge there were no supervisors to talk to. I was afraid to call scheduling again and tell them to use the reserve that was sitting on the recliner as a stand by. I felt like I had no support from scheduling after the conversation I had with them earlier. I literally dragged myself to the briefing and could barely talk for fear of throwing up. I was a mess! My flight attendant in charge asked me if I was going to make it, I replied, I have no choice.

By the time the supervisor showed up, it was too late, I was already on the airplane. The only lucky thing that happened to me was that I was assigned D-zone on the L10-11. Fortunately for me, I was right next to the restrooms in the back of the airplane (D-zone). Before and after takeoff I was fighting not to get sick. I couldn't concentrate on what I was doing and the worse thing about it was I had to work D-zone alone.

I remember feeling sweaty and light headed when I was serving the passengers, nevertheless, I persevered and finished my service. Believe it or not I was able to control my upset stomach until we landed.

Just as the captain put on the brakes I immediately jumped out of my jump seat and ran to the restroom, I couldn't hold it any longer! I don't have to describe what happened next. I'll leave it to your imagination.

I went to the front of the aircraft and informed the A-line what happened to me. She suggested I call flight operations and get off the trip. That's exactly what I did and operations booked me on the next flight home without detailed questions. That's how it should be in every company, if you tell someone that you're very sick there should be no question of your inability to work. You should never have to sacrifice your health because someone threatens your record.

This is what I'm talking about, the little things you don't know about as a new employee. Scheduling won't tell you what you should do, they want you to work! Don't forget, you have supervisors to help you. Use your own judgment if this should happen to you but I recommend that you don't fly when you're sick.

I hope this chapter has given you the inside scoop of what really goes on behind closed doors.

Remember you're the only one who knows if this is the job for you!

So as I've said from the beginning, *Follow Your Dreams!*

Survival Story:

How I Survived the New York Trade Center Bombing.

As a flight attendant, you may experience situations beyond your control. You may even find yourself in a life threatening situation, just as I did one grey February morning.

In the month of February 1993, I decided to bid for call in reserve so that I could hold weekends off. My seniority wouldn't allow me to hold weekends off on a regular line so reserve was the next best thing.

Unfortunately, this opened the door for me to receive trips I normally wouldn't fly as a line holder. When I called scheduling to receive my trip they told me that I was going to New York City and that I was flying A-line. I was very excited because the trip had a long layover at the Vista Hotel and that would give me the opportunity to visit the Twin Towers. The Vista Hotel sat between the Twin Towers.

When I got to the flight lounge, I pulled up the trip and called for a briefing. My crew met me in the briefing room and we discussed the trip and details of the flight. We were all excited about the Trade Center and talked about getting together and touring the sights.

After the briefing was over we headed upstairs to meet the airplane. I went up to the gate agent and asked for the pre-departure report, then headed down the jet-way. The girls and I began preparing the cabin for boarding and after everyone settled in their seats, I made an announcement and received the final departure list from the gate agent. We were on our way to New York City!

After a long night of flying we finally arrived in New York. We were tired and ready to get to the hotel. On the way to the hotel the crew and I talked about getting together in the morning and having breakfast. We also discussed touring the Twin Towers after lunch. It was late by the time we got to the hotel, so we decided to call it a night. We all signed in at the desk and headed to our rooms for a good night sleep.

The next morning I got up feeling very tired and something told me to stay in my room and have breakfast instead of meeting the crew. I called one of the girls and explained that I didn't feel up to touring the Twin Towers and that I was going to rest in my room.

I called room service and placed my order, then laid on the couch and watched television. Later that morning, I started preparing for departure and began picking up my things around the room, making sure that I had everything. It was getting late so I grabbed a couple of towels and went into the bathroom to take a shower. I got out of the shower and put on my sweats and then began blow drying my hair.

After a few minutes, I went out to the living room area to change the channel on the television, when all of a sudden there was a loud Bang! It shook the ground with so much force, it nearly knocked me off my feet. As I stood there in shock fearing for more explosions, I looked up to the window and began hearing screams. A couple of minutes passed, then suddenly I noticed black smoke pouring into my room from under the door.

Simultaneously, the hotel alarm went off and someone began shouting on the hotel speaker, *"**Everyone Get Out! This Is Not A Drill! Please Evacuate the Building!**"*

I grabbed my shoes but couldn't tie my shoelaces because my hands were shaking uncontrollably. Frantically, I looked around the room and noticed my wedding ring sitting on the dresser. I ran over and picked it up then placed it on my finger, I wasn't about to leave that behind! I then went out into the hallway, to see if anyone else was out there. I couldn't believe the smoke in the hallway, I couldn't see anything. I then called out, "Is anyone out here, hey! Is anyone here?" Strangely as it sounds, no one responded to me.

I ran back into my room to see if I could get anything else to bring with me. At that time I was thinking... I'm sure we'll be able to come back in and get our things later. They probably just want us out of the building for the time being......... So then I thought I needed to get out of the room because the smoke was getting worse.

I then grabbed my raincoat and shut my hotel door and started running down the hall and met up with some people that were running the opposite of me saying, "Don't go this way, it's not an exit." We all took off running down the hall looking for any exit. In the smoke, we gathered with other people who were looking for the exit as well. It was so hard to see through the smoke but finally we saw a red light above the door, "Exit."

We all went through and started running down the stairs, it was so frightening! I grabbed this lady who seemed like she was having a hard time getting down the stairs, so I asked her if she was all right. She replied, "No I'm not," so I held onto her and we both hurried down the dark smoky stairs together.

People were running by us crying and yelling down the stairs in a panic. We finally got to the bottom of the stairs and we pushed open the emergency door and were confronted by a cold blast of air. As we ran out the door, the ground was covered with ice and people were falling all around me.

The lady I was with thanked me for helping her, and then she disappeared into the crowd. I was alone. At first I didn't know where to go. I started running away from the burning building towards the hotel across the street from the Vista. Clutching my coat, I tried to keep the wind from holding me back. It had just begun to snow. My feet were slipping on the ice as I struggled to get away.

I began to hear banging noises behind me and I turned around to see people trapped in the Twin Towers, screaming and yelling for help. They were breaking the windows so they could breathe. The black smoke was billowing out the windows and doors of the Vista Hotel and Twin Towers.

Fire rescue and policemen were everywhere, all the streets were blocked off. Someone shouted, "Come this way, there's a building we can go into for shelter," so I ran towards the building to the right of the Vista. Inside the building people from the hotel gathered and desperately walked around looking for loved ones.

I was trying to find the girls I was flying with. It was very confusing pushing through the crowd. Suddenly, someone starts yelling, "Get out of the building! The building is on fire!" Then firemen entered the building telling us to evacuate. I couldn't believe it, I survived the Vista fire now I have to survive this fire too. I decided that I needed to venture out myself and find protection, so I ran across the street to the Millennium Hotel.

Just as I stepped onto the sidewalk in front of the large hotel, someone yelled my name. I looked up to find one of my co-workers, I couldn't believe we had found each other. I told her that I was on my way into the hotel to call Delta. We decided that she would search for the other girls because they were touring the Twin Towers when the explosion had happened and I would set everything up for us at the hotel. After standing in line for quite some time to use the pay phone, I called operations and told them the story. At first they didn't know what I was talking about. I had to repeat myself several times before they got the picture. They told me to stay at the hotel and wait for Delta to set us up there. Delta was very understanding through the whole ordeal and set us up quickly.

I went up to my room and turned on the news in hopes of finding out what happened. It was then that I found out that terrorists had tried to bring the Twin Towers down by placing a bomb in the garage beneath the Vista Hotel. However, they were not successful due to lack of knowledge.

I tried to call my husband but couldn't get through because all the phone lines were busy.

Several minutes later, I received a phone call from a supervisor in Salt Lake City, who specialized in terrorist situations. We discussed what happened and she gave me support and expressed the desire to assist us in anyway. After the phone call there was a knock on the door. I got up and opened the door to find three smiling faces, thank God she found them, and they survived! We all hugged and sat on the bed in disbelief of what just occurred.

Finally, I got a hold of my husband; he told me that a supervisor from Salt Lake City had paged him about the situation. He wanted to fly to New York to be with me but I told him that would be difficult because all the streets were blocked off and fire and rescue were not letting anyone in the area. I told him that I would call him later, after I settled in for the night.

The girls and I realized that we had to go back to the Vista Hotel to get our belongings, so we went downstairs in the lobby and began asking questions regarding our luggage. Everyone walked around in a daze, and some people were crying as they huddled in-groups.

We walked outside and headed towards the Vista Hotel. It was a difficult task, walking past all the destruction. We were walking over fire hoses and the smell of smoke was tremendous. As we approached the Vista Hotel, there was a policeman standing at the front of the building. We asked him if we could get our luggage from inside the hotel. He told us that we might be able to come back later. He wasn't sure when they were going to allow people back into the building to retrieve their items.

Frustrated, we walked around to the front of the lobby, in search of more information.

As we entered the Vista Hotel lobby, the stench of burnt debris smothered us as we stepped over fire hoses and pieces of the lobby that were hurled through the air by the explosion. The entire lobby was black and dripping with water because of the fire hoses. I turned to my right and discovered a huge whole in the lobby floor where the bomb had penetrated through. My mouth dropped to the floor, as I viewed the destruction left behind by the explosion.

Suddenly, a fireman shouted to us, "Hey, what are you doing in here?" "Sir" we replied, "Can you tell us when we might be able to retrieve our luggage?" He replied, "Not tonight!" He explained that the hotel had received severe fire and structural damage and it would be impossible for anyone to gather personal belongings under these circumstances, so we left.

On the way back to our new hotel, I had flashbacks of all the events that took place. I could smell the smoke, feel the impact, hear the sirens, and most of all see the images left behind from the explosion. My heart sank! I thanked God that he spared me from being killed in the explosion.

When we got inside the lobby, there were people everywhere trying to find out information about the bombing. Everyone was in shock and in disbelief of what just occurred. There were people waiting in line to use the pay phone to call their families.

The front desk was swamped with evacuees trying to get a room for the night. There were people huddled together crying and consoling each other. The atmosphere was intense and full of confusion as people wandered around helplessly, looking for answers. Unfortunately, no one heard anything about when we would be able to go back to the Vista Hotel and gather our belongings. Most of the people did not have their suitcases with them because just like us they had left them behind thinking they would be able to return for them later.

Eventually, we realized that we were not going to get our things so we headed upstairs to our rooms. The hotel employees did their best to make us feel comfortable. They even left us a basket of personal items in our bathrooms. Later, we all met downstairs in the restaurant and had dinner. Delta was kind enough to provide a tab for us because we had no money. After we ate dinner we headed back to our rooms to try and get some sleep. I had a difficult time falling asleep. I kept hearing the sound of the explosion in my head and was fearful that there might be another bombing. I was in my bed with the covers over my head, hoping I was safe. It was the longest night of my life.

Around 10:00 p.m. I received a phone call from one of the girls and to my surprise she told me that they wanted to go home on the first flight out the next morning. She said that they didn't want to stay in New York anymore. I asked, "What about your luggage, don't you want to get your belongings?" She replied, "No, I just want to get out of here." I said okay and told her I would try to get her luggage from the Vista Hotel for her. I had made up my mind that I was staying to get my things. I was glad at least one of the girls stayed behind with me so I wasn't alone.

The next morning there was a note under my door saying we were finally able to get our belongings from the Vista Hotel, boy was I happy!

We got ready and went down the street to the Sheraton Hotel where the Red Cross was set up to assist anyone who left their things behind.

We went up to the table where representatives of the Red Cross were sitting and signed our names on a list. This way the Red Cross could go into the Vista Hotel and retrieve our things. They told us the building was so unsafe that they had volunteers from the Red Cross go into the building, to retrieve items in the dark. They were actually using flashlights to help them find their way. They were going room by room looking for survivors.

The day dragged on and we were growing weary. Unfortunately, we were one of the last to get our suitcases. I was pacing the floor trying to think of a way to speed things up because our time was running out. We had less than a couple of hours to make the flight back home. I went out to the curb and saw a man from the Red Cross so I grabbed him and said, "Please sir, can you help us? We are desperate to get our belongings so we can make the last flight home to Salt Lake City." He thought for a minute and said "Okay give me a few minutes and I'll personally go to your room and get your suitcases." I thanked him.

He then turned around and headed back to the Vista Hotel. I watched him as he hurried towards the hotel and I said a prayer.

It seemed like forever, I kept going out to the curb to look for him. I was thinking, where is he, did he find our things? Looking at my watch I began to pace the floor and decided to wait out on the curb for him. I stood out there waiting for his return, then suddenly from a distance, I saw him. He had suitcases on his back and around his arms, he was actually running down the street so that we could make our flight.

I was overwhelmed. When he approached us, I hugged him and started to cry. I thanked him and desperately looked around for a taxi.

We had our things and were ready to go! Out of the blue a taxi pulled up right where I was standing. I yelled, right here! We need a ride to the airport fast! He jumped out of the car and put our suitcases in the trunk then we took off like a bat out of hell. We told him the story on the way to the airport and he was amazed.

Finally, we got to the airport, I was hoping it wasn't too late. We grabbed our luggage and started running down the terminal towards the gate.

I looked up and noticed three gate agents getting ready for final departure at our gate. We ran up to them and told them who we were and what had happened to us. We told them we were dressed in jeans and sweatshirts because our uniforms were covered in soot and reeked of smoke. Considering what we had just been through they had no problem with it and they escorted us onto the airplane.

After we settled in the flight attendants working the flight all gathered around us to hear the frightening story. I got up and went to the galley to get a glass of water and tried to unwind.

I peeked around the corner and saw a red coat gate agent walking quickly down the isle. She came into the galley and asked who I was. Then she asked me why I was dressed like that in a rude tone. My nerves were already fried; just the tone of her voice made me start shaking. I nervously tried to tell her that our uniforms were ruined and we had no other clothes. I told her that Delta knew about it but she didn't seem to care. She made some comment then turned around and headed back up the isle towards the door.

The flight attendants came over and consoled us after her rude comments about our clothing. I was furious over the way she treated us after all we had been through, she actually made my co-worker cry.

On the way home, I wrote her up regarding her attitude. It was a long ride home, of course I couldn't sleep so I went to the galley and talked to the flight crew. By the time we got home it was around midnight. We were told earlier that a supervisor from Delta would greet us and take us downstairs to the flight lounge where we could discuss what had happened to us in New

York. Unfortunately, no one was there when we arrived, so we went home.

The next day, I was feeling terrible. I spoke to my supervisor and was given a couple days off after the awful event.

I went back to work without any type of debriefing, counseling or group therapy. I believe that Delta should have set up a group session for the survivors of the bombing. It was hard to go back to work without thinking about the explosion and all the events that took place. I felt very alone. I didn't go back to New York for along time and had no desire to.

I avoided all the trips that flew into New York and went back to flying a line instead of call in reserve. It's to risky being on reserve, they can send you anywhere and you never know what can happen, like what happened to us in New York.

I think what helped me survive the tragedy was the emergency training I received through Delta. You are trained to handle events, there's a class you must attend that teaches terrorist acts and security procedures. In this job you have to be prepared for anything!

I talked to one of the flight attendants weeks later and she appeared to be handling it as best as she could. I never had the opportunity to express my true feelings and who knows if the girls were really all right.

As the days went on I grew more and more tired and could still feel the affects of the tragedy.

As the years passed, I realized that I could no longer fulfill my duties as a flight attendant. I felt it was time for me to move on with my life and fulfill other dreams.

I'm grateful that I survived the bombing and thankful that I was able to fulfill my dream as a flight attendant.

The End.

Biography: Tamara L. Clark

At the tender age of seven, I was fortunate to have had my first flight on PSA. The flight attendants onboard took very good care of me and soon became apart of my life. I traveled back and forth from Los Angeles to San Diego on a DC-9 in the late sixties and became familiar with the routine. Flying was already in my blood!

On one of my flights to Los Angeles, I asked the flight attendant if I could pass out the mints. Impressed by my desires she agreed and walked behind me as I passed out the mints to the passengers. Everyone thought I was cute, wearing my Girl Scout uniform and passing out the mints, I received compliments and tips from the passengers. One man gave me a quarter for my efforts.

Later in my life, I began preparing for the position. I attended college and worked part-time in a department store. At the age of twenty-two I had my first interview with Republic Airlines. The interview was a good experience for me, however two weeks later I was notified that I wasn't being considered for the job. I had several more interviews but it wasn't to be in my life at that time. After years of interviewing, I was finally hired by Delta Airlines. Even after all the rejections, I never gave up! I knew that I would never be truly happy until I fulfilled my life long dream. So, do as I did and follow your dreams!